Contents

The Light Ahead

IT WAS A DARK night in 1898 and, besides the sound of the rain beating against the glass roof, everything was quiet. Marie and Pierre Curie stood inside the entrance to their laboratory at the University of Paris. It was late, but they couldn't resist coming back to the small, cold shed where they worked together during the day. They wanted just one more look at their new discovery. It was bitterly cold because the little stove had burned out hours ago, but all Marie and Pierre could feel was excitement.

BELOW: *Pierre and Marie Curie in their laboratory in 1900, with the measuring instruments Pierre had developed to measure radioactivity.*

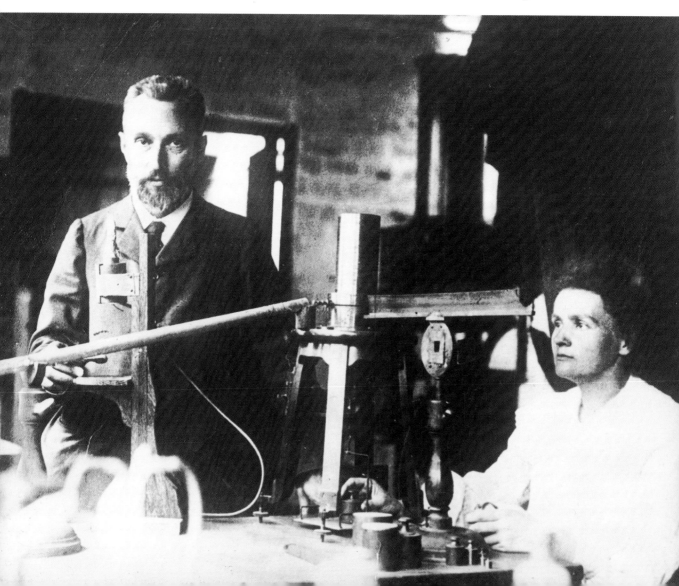

For many months now, Marie and Pierre had been working long hours in their freezing laboratory. Together they had been trying to find the source of radioactivity. Eventually they found a radioactive element which they named polonium.

A Strange Glow

Marie and Pierre knew how important their discovery was to science, but there was also something completely fascinating about their element and it was only at night that they could really enjoy its magic. The test tube resting in the rack on the table, which contained polonium mixed with water, glowed with a shimmer of light. The laboratory was thrown into shadow, but through the glow, Pierre could just make out the excitement on Marie's face. All the hard work had been worth it!

In 1898, Marie and Pierre Curie discovered two new radioactive elements: polonium and radium. There was great excitement at their discovery, and radium was soon hailed as a new cure for cancer and other illnesses. The discovery of polonium and radium was just the beginning of human understanding of radioactivity. It would be many years before people realized the dangers of radioactivity, too. Marie became the first woman to win a Nobel Prize and the only person to win two Nobels.

RIGHT: *Marie Curie handled radioactive elements without gloves or protective clothing. People did not know then that polonium and radium could harm people.*

IN THEIR OWN WORDS

'Our products containing concentrated radium were all spontaneously luminous [shining out light].
My husband, who had hoped to see them show beautiful colourations, had to agree that this other characteristic gave him even greater satisfaction.'

MARIE CURIE IN *PIERRE CURIE*, PUBLISHED IN 1923.

SCIENCE IN THE NINETEENTH CENTURY

The nineteenth century was a time of great discoveries. Many of the everyday things that we now take for granted, such as electricity, the telephone, the motor car and photography were invented then. There were huge developments in medicine and a growing understanding of disease too. In 1864, the French scientist Louis Pasteur discovered that microscopic organisms in the air caused milk to go sour. This led him to discover the causes of the illnesses anthrax and rabies. In Britain in 1865, Joseph Lister realized that micro-organisms in the air also caused infections in surgery. He went on to develop antiseptic surgery. Once-deadly diseases or medical conditions could now be cured. All around the world, scientists were making new discoveries, which would improve the lives and health of everyone. There was an air of excitement as they raced to find the next 'big thing'.

BELOW: *The physicist Wilhelm Röntgen, who stumbled upon X-rays by accident while working on special glass tubes.*

X-rays

On 8 November 1895, a German physicist called Wilhelm Röntgen, (pronounced VIL-helm REHNT-guhn) made a discovery that would affect both science and medicine: he discovered X-rays. Röntgen found that if he passed an electric current through a glass tube, it could give out invisible rays. Röntgen called these rays X-rays, because he didn't know what they were at first. Röntgen asked his wife to hold a photographic plate and directed X-rays on to her hand. The result was astounding: the first X-ray photograph, showing the bones of the human hand. By January 1896, X-rays were already being used in hospitals and they caught the attention of other scientists, including the young physicist Marie Curie, who wondered how else these rays could be used.

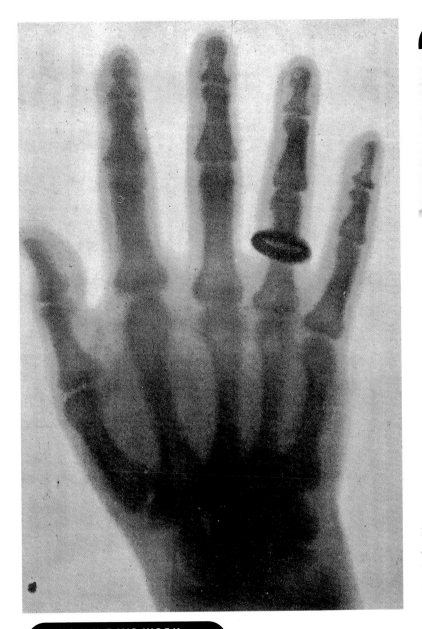

IN THEIR OWN WORDS

'Nothing in life is to be feared. It is only to be understood.'

MARIE CURIE.

LEFT: *The first X-ray photograph, showing the hand of Röntgen's wife. The skeleton of her hand and the ring on her third finger are clearly visible.*

HOW X-RAYS WORK

X-rays rays pass through soft material, such as flesh, but are stopped by solid material such as bone or metal. If a photographic plate is put behind something and X-rays are shone at it, the rays produce an image on the plate behind. The image is a shadow of the solid material.

The Early Years

MARIE CURIE (pronounced KYOO-ree) was born Marya Sklodowska (pronounced sklaw-DAWF-skah) on 7 November 1867. She was born on the outskirts of Warsaw, the capital city of Poland. The youngest of five children, Marya had an elder brother, Jozef, and three elder sisters, Zofia, Bronislawa and Helena. Her family lived next door to the private girls' school, where Maria's mother was headmistress.

Marya's father was also a teacher, who passed on his love of science to his children.

ABOVE: *Freta Street in Warsaw, Poland, in 1819. Marya was born in the building on the left with the balcony.*

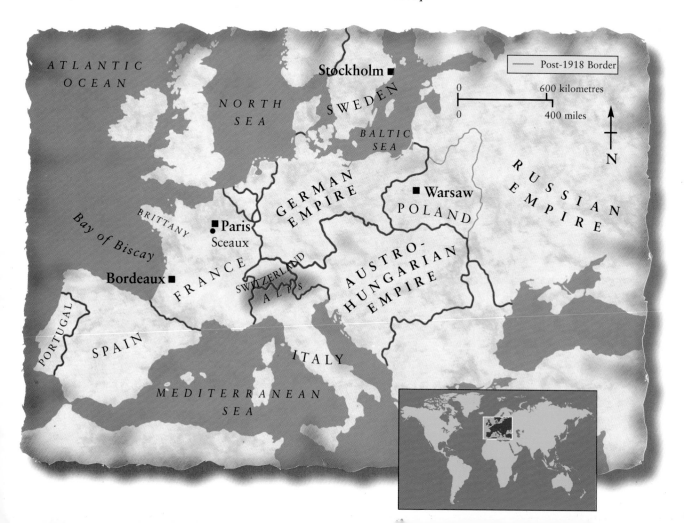

RIGHT: *Marya, aged about sixteen, poses for a school photograph. Although she enjoyed her studies, Marie disliked the Russian teachers, who were harder on the Polish students.*

Marya particularly enjoyed the way her father talked about nature. However, his passion for education eventually got him into trouble. Since the late eighteenth century, Poland had been governed by Russia, and the Russian authorities tried to stamp out all traces of Polish culture. They were afraid that people like Marya's father might teach his pupils too much about Polish culture, so he was made to give up his job. This meant the family suddenly had very little money.

Forced to move into ever-smaller houses, the family struggled to make ends meet. But the children were still encouraged to do well in their studies. Marya's father would often read to his children, particularly Polish poetry and literature (which was banned), and they all grew up with a thirst for knowledge and education, which both parents encouraged in their children. Marya studied hard at school and showed signs of outstanding intelligence.

In 1874, when Marya was seven, tragedy struck. She lost her sister Zofia to typhus and, four years later, her mother died from tuberculosis. Their deaths hit Marya hard and she became very depressed, but she managed to keep up her studies. By the age of nine she was top of her class, and at the age of fifteen she won a gold medal. In 1883, when she was sixteen, Marya's father sent her away for a year to live with relatives on a farm. At last Marya began to enjoy life again.

IN THEIR OWN WORDS

'I can still see little Maniusia (Marya), a plump girl with fair, curly hair bound up with a black velvet ribbon, wearing her apron trimmed with flounces; her eyes were pale grey and they looked at the world with a smile, kindness and unusual seriousness. Although the youngest, she influenced her classmates with her unusual intelligence, abilities and great memory...'

MARIE'S SISTER HELENA, WRITING ABOUT MARYA, IN HER MEMOIRS.

THE QUEST FOR EDUCATION

In 1885, aged eighteen, Marya returned to Warsaw, refreshed and hungry for more education. At that time, women were not allowed to go to university in Poland. But Marya and her elder sister Bronia were determined to carry on studying, even if it meant going abroad to the famous Sorbonne, the University of Paris. But there was a big problem: lack of money. Marya decided that she'd have to earn her own money by giving lessons from home.

Marya's free time was spent reading and attending secret meetings of the 'Flying University'. This was a women's club with about 1,000 members, who met regularly to attend lectures by famous Polish scientists,

IN THEIR OWN WORDS

'I was as much interested in literature and sociology as in science... however, during those years of isolated work, trying little by little to find my real preferences, I finally turned towards mathematics and physics, and resolutely undertook a serious preparation for future work...'

MARYA, WRITING ABOUT HER GROWING INTEREST IN SCIENCE IN A LETTER TO HER COUSIN, HENRIETTA MICHATOWSKA, IN ABOUT 1888.

historians and writers. The Russians would have banned these meetings if they had known, but despite the danger of arrest, for Marya it was her chance to carry on with her studies and mix with other intelligent women.

A Passport to University

In 1885, Marya and Bronia thought of a way to pay for both of them to go to university in Paris. Bronia would go to university, while Marya earned money as a governess to support her through university. Then, once Bronia had qualified and got a job, she would support Marya through her studies.

LEFT: *Marya's family gather for a family photograph in 1890. From the left: Marya, her father, Bronia and Helena.*

LEFT: *Marya (left) and Bronia (right). Marya often wanted to leave her post as a governess, but the 'deal' with Bronia stopped her from giving up.*

Becoming a governess wasn't an easy decision for Marya, but it was one of the few ways for penniless women with an education to make a living in Poland. She became a governess of the Zorawski family, working long hours looking after their two youngest daughters (Andzia, aged ten, and Bronka, aged eighteen) for very little pay.

Perhaps one of the most difficult parts of her job was living in another household and obeying their rules. Marya didn't enjoy her job, but it was her passport to university, and in her spare time she still managed to study and decide what she wanted to do in the future.

IN THEIR OWN WORDS

'I am learning chemistry from a book... you can imagine how little I get out of that, but what can I do, as I have no place to make experiments or do practical work?'

MARYA, WRITING ABOUT HER GROWING FRUSTRATIONS AS A GOVERNESS, IN A LETTER TO HER BROTHER JOZEF, IN OCTOBER 1888.

Paris

IN NOVEMBER 1891, when she was twenty-three, Marya arrived in Paris to live with her sister Bronia and her brother-in-law, and start her studies at the Sorbonne. By now she was a serious young woman, slight and rather shy, with intelligent grey eyes and curly fair hair. A forty-hour train journey separated her from her beloved Poland and the rest of her family. She was one of many Polish women who went to Paris in search of further education. They couldn't have arrived at a more exciting time.

The years 1880 to 1914 are often called the *belle époque*, which is French for 'a time of peace and prosperity'. In 1891, Marya was not wealthy, but she found herself enjoying

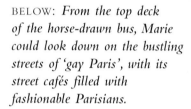

BELOW: *From the top deck of the horse-drawn bus, Marie could look down on the bustling streets of 'gay Paris', with its street cafés filled with fashionable Parisians.*

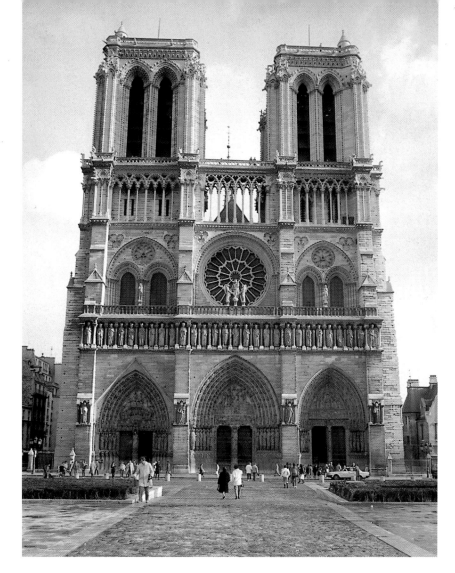

LEFT: *The Gothic cathedral of Notre Dame. With its carved exterior and magnificent, stained-glass windows, Notre Dame is one of the most beautiful buildings in Paris.*

a sense of freedom in Paris. After life under Russian rule and years as a governess, for once she was on her own. One of the first things she did was take the French spelling of her name – Marya became Marie.

As a foreigner, Marie was less restricted than French women living in Paris at this time. Young French women had to be accompanied by chaperones when they went out in public, but Marie came and went as she pleased. She could take a bus to the heart of the city to see the impressive Notre Dame cathedral, or the magnificent Arc de Triomphe.

IN THEIR OWN WORDS

'All that I saw and learned that was new delighted me. It was like a new world opened to me, the world of science, which I was at last permitted to know at all liberty.'

MARIE CURIE IN *PIERRE CURIE*, PUBLISHED IN 1923.

THE CENTRE OF SCIENCE

To be a science student at the Sorbonne in 1891 was exceptional, but for a woman it was groundbreaking. French women were not taught physics or chemistry at school, so they were unable to study science at university. Of the 1,825 students at the Sorbonne, only twenty-three were women.

Educational reforms in France were focused on raising the standard of science study and the Sorbonne was at the very centre of change. New laboratories and classrooms were being built, and a selection of brilliant and inspirational scientists were employed as professors. Marie was taught by some of the greatest physicists of the age, including Gabriel Lippmann (who won a Nobel Prize in 1908 for his work on colour photography).

ABOVE: *The grand exterior of the Sorbonne, the University of Paris.*

BELOW: *Women attend a physics lecture at the Sorbonne in 1867.*

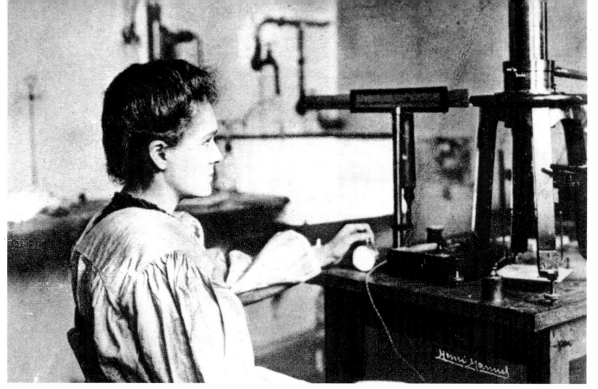

Now that Marie was finally where she wanted to be, she buried herself in books and studied hard. She even found it difficult to find time for new friends. It wasn't long before she decided to move out of Bronia's house too, because the constant interruptions of family life stopped her working as hard as she would like. Marie found a room at the top of a six-storey block of flats. It was cheap because it was small and unfurnished. It was also cold, with just a small stove to cook simple food. Marie didn't mind too much. She enjoyed her independence and she loved the views of Paris from her top-floor room.

Two years later, in 1893, Marie came first in her year in the *licence des sciences* (science degree). The following year she came second in her class in the *licence des mathematiques* (maths degree). Marie had proved she could succeed in the male-dominated scientific world of the nineteenth century.

IN THEIR OWN WORDS

Ideals flood this tiny room;
They led her to this
foreign land;
They urge her to
pursue the truth
And seek the light that's close at hand.

It is the light she longs to find,
When she delights in learning more.
Her world is learning; it defines
The destiny she's reaching for.

AN EXCERPT FROM A POEM WRITTEN BY MARIE, ORIGINALLY IN POLISH IN ABOUT 1892, TO HER FRIEND JADWIGA DYDYNSKA.

Partners in Science

WHEN MARIE MET Pierre Curie at a physicist's house in the spring of 1894, she was filled with admiration. Pierre was thirty-five, and a teacher and scientist at the *Ecole de Physique* (School of Physics) at the Sorbonne. Like Marie, Pierre had been raised by a poor but educated family. His father and grandfather were doctors, and Pierre had studied at home with his brother Jacques, who was also a physicist. He was quiet and serious, passionate about science but with a love of the countryside and the simple life. Pierre was as taken with Marie as she was with him. He had found a rare woman who could share his world – the world of science. A few months into their friendship, Pierre asked Marie to marry him.

By the time Pierre met Marie, he had already made a name for himself in scientific circles. His experiments with crystals and magnetism were important and he also invented some scientific measuring instruments, for which he'd been highly praised. Yet his salary was very low and he lived at home with his parents.

BELOW: *'Women of genius are rare' wrote Pierre Curie in his diary before he met Marie. He never believed he'd meet a woman with whom he could share his life and work.*

IN THEIR OWN WORDS

'His speech, rather slow and deliberate, his simplicity, and his smile, at once grave and youthful, inspired confidence.'

MARIE, WRITING IN HER JOURNAL ABOUT MEETING PIERRE FOR THE FIRST TIME.

After a year's courtship, Marie and Pierre were married in 1895. The wedding was held at the town hall in Sceaux, on the outskirts of Paris, where Pierre's family lived. The sun shone, and her father and sister Helena came from Poland to celebrate the big day. Later, Marie and Pierre headed off on their new bicycles for a honeymoon in Brittany. Cycling had just started to become popular as a way of keeping fit. This was to be the first of Marie and Pierre's cycling adventures in the French countryside. In the years to come, these trips were to become a welcome relief from long hours spent in the laboratory.

ABOVE: *The newly-wed Pierre and Marie pose beside their bicycles in the garden of Pierre's parents. Marie is wearing cycling culottes, which were quite daring for the time.*

ABOVE: *Marie and Pierre with their first daughter Irène, in 1903.*

A NEW HOME

Marie and Pierre's first home was a small flat, with furniture they had been given by their families. Marie did the cooking and most of the housework herself, which was unusual for a woman in her position at that time. She also continued to study towards becoming a schoolteacher, because unlike many women of her time, Marie didn't believe a family should be supported by her husband's salary alone.

Pierre's promotion at the *Ecole de Physique* in September 1895 meant they had a little more money, but the Curies still had to be careful about how much they spent. Marie's carefully kept records of their expenses reveal that the only luxuries the Curies allowed themselves at this time were bicycle accessories.

Motherhood and Science

In September 1897, Marie and Pierre had their first child, a daughter they named Irène. Marie employed a childminder so that she could get back to her work at the laboratory. There was something in particular that she wanted to research…

After the discovery of X-rays in 1895, a year later another scientist, Antoine Henri Becquerel (pronounced bek-uh-REHL) discovered that uranium ore gave off similar rays. Marie decided that these rays needed investigating. Nobody realized that understanding uranium rays would become more important than the discovery of X-rays. Uranium's major use at that time was as a colouring for glazing pottery.

RIGHT: *Antoine Henri Becquerel discovered that uranium gave off rays by accident. After leaving uranium exposed to light on top of a photographic plate, he noticed a faint image of the element on the plate below.*

Great Discoveries

IN THE WINTER of 1897, Marie started investigating uranium as part of her Ph.D. dissertation. The cramped old storerooms at the *Ecole de Physique* became her laboratory and since she had little money for equipment, she started her investigations using a measuring instrument invented by Pierre.

First of all, Marie measured the amount of rays given off by uranium ore, which she called 'emissions'. She invented the word 'radioactive' to describe any material that gave off these emissions. Then she started to test other materials, to see if were also radioactive.

Mystery Elements

On 17 February 1898, Marie found that a compound called pitchblende produced greater emissions than pure uranium. This convinced her that it must contain other elements, which were more radioactive than uranium. Marie realized that these were elements that hadn't been discovered before. She had to extract the elements, to prove to the science world that they really existed.

Marie discussed her findings with Pierre, who was becoming increasingly interested in his wife's work. Pierre had just been turned down for a top position at the Sorbonne. Marie's discovery helped him to forget his rejection and he

LEFT: *Marie and Pierre in their laboratory in Paris, where they made their great discoveries.*

To find the mystery elements in the pitchblende, Marie and Pierre had to break down the substance to isolate, or extract, the ingredients. First, the pitchblende had to be ground down and then sieved, a kilogramme at a time. Then the pitchblende was stirred for hours as it boiled down to form a liquid that could be distilled. Finally, this liquid was electrolyzed and tiny amounts of the radioactive elements were isolated.

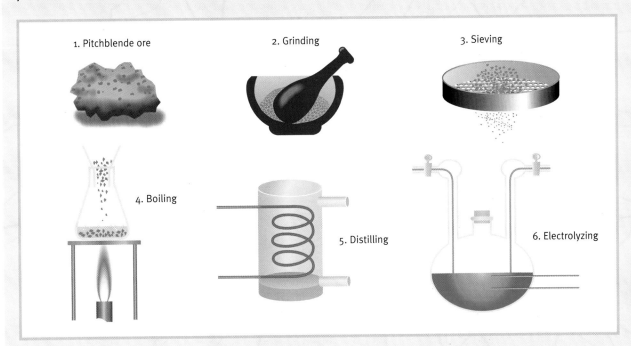

1. Pitchblende ore

2. Grinding

3. Sieving

4. Boiling

5. Distilling

6. Electrolyzing

dropped his own work to help her extract the mystery elements. However, extracting them was difficult. Pitchblende looks a little like coal. It would arrive at the laboratory in great sacks, out of which Marie and Pierre had to find tiny amounts of the mystery elements.

Discovering Polonium

The work was long and tiring, but Marie was never fazed by the task before her. Eventually, in the spring of 1898, Marie and Pierre extracted one of the radioactive elements. They named it polonium after Poland, Marie's beloved homeland.

'We thus believe that the substance we have extracted from pitchblende contains a metal never known before.... If the existence of this metal is confirmed, we propose to call it polonium, after the name of the country of origin of one of us.'

MARIE AND PIERRE CURIE IN THE LABORATORY NOTEBOOKS, JULY 1898.

DISCOVERING RADIUM

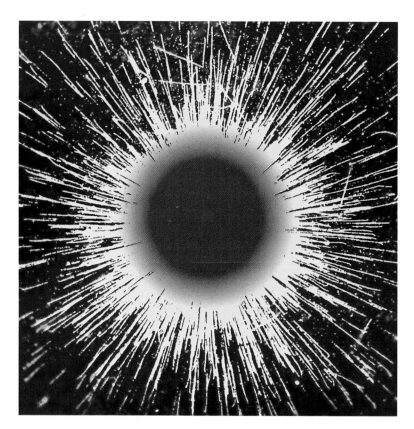

LEFT: *You cannot normally see radioactivity, but when a speck of radium is placed on a special photographic plate, bright yellow tracks appear. This is radioactivity.*

After the discovery of polonium, all the hard work must have seemed worth it. However, the excitement about polonium was short-lived because there appeared to be another mystery element in the pitchblende, which was even more radioactive. Marie was determined to extract this element.

In the search for what later became known as radium, the process of extraction continued for nearly four years. Tonnes of pitchblende needed to be treated to isolate just a fraction of a gramme of radium. Sometimes Pierre thought they would lose the battle, but it was Marie who insisted they carried on.

IN THEIR OWN WORDS

'I had to work with as much as 20 kilograms of material at a time.... It was exhausting work to move the containers about, to transfer the liquids, and to stir for hours at a time, with an iron bar, the boiling material in the cast-iron basin.'

MARIE CURIE IN *PIERRE CURIE*, PUBLISHED IN 1923.

Throughout these years, the Curies still struggled for money. They both had to find teaching work to make ends meet and Pierre made a further unsuccessful application to the Sorbonne. To escape from the laboratory, they took to the countryside or to the coast. Walking, cycling, enjoying nature and watching their little girl grow up brought them a lot of joy. Then in May 1902, Marie's father died, and she was devastated. The triumph of isolating pure radium just a few months later must have been something she wished she could have shared with him.

In July 1902, Marie's determination paid off when she announced to the world that they had finally isolated one decigramme (0.1 gramme) of radium. It might have weighed less than a potato crisp, but it was a great achievement.

Mysterious Properties

Radium fascinated scientists with its many mysterious properties. Not only did it give out a bluish light, called phosphorescence, it also gave off heat. It was heavier than lead and it discoloured test tubes, turning them slightly purple. More alarmingly, it burned the skin, but without any of the pain associated with burns. The Curies were delighted with the element's unusual behaviour and would mail out samples containing radium to other scientists for them to enjoy. In the early days, Pierre even took a small test tube of the substance to parties, to amaze the other guests.

BELOW: *A cartoon in the magazine* Vanity Fair, *showing Marie and Pierre's discovery of radium.*

NOBEL PRIZE

In June 1903, Marie's research earned her the Ph.D. she had strived for. Then in November, a letter arrived for the Curies from the Swedish Academy in Stockholm. The letter revealed that Marie and Pierre, together with Henri Becquerel, were the winners of the Nobel Prize for Physics, for 1903. Behind the scenes, the selection of a woman had not been an easy decision for the judges at the academy. Many scientists who nominated the winners chose to ignore Marie Curie's work. In a male-dominated, scientific world, they preferred the glory to go to Pierre. Fortunately, other scientists disagreed and the Curies were both recognized for their work on radioactivity and uranium.

BELOW: *A drawing showing Pierre Curie collecting the Davy Medal for discovering radium, in 1903. This medal was given to scientists in memory of Sir Humphry Davy (1778–1829), the English scientist who invented the miner's safety lamp.*

LEFT: *This coin was made to celebrate Marie and Pierre's discovery of radium and the Nobel Prize they won in 1903.*

The Curies couldn't make the trip to Sweden to accept the prize because they were too ill, but the Nobel Prize brought them fame. Virtually unknown outside science circles in France, let alone the world, the media directed its attention on the quiet and publicity-shy couple. Newspapers were intrigued by their relationship. The notion of a husband and wife working as a professional team was extraordinary at that time. French journalists called at their flat for interviews, but the Curies didn't like the invasion of their privacy. Pierre and Marie just wanted to carry on as before and continue with their research.

The Nobel Prize did bring them more money, although they gave much of it away to their families and poor students. The money helped them to carry on with their work in better conditions and to employ another laboratory assistant. At home, they redecorated their flat and installed a modern bathroom.

IN THEIR OWN WORDS

'I wish you good health and success for all your family – and also that you may never be submerged by such a correspondence as inundates us at this moment... I regret a little that I threw away the letters we received... There were sonnets and poems on radium, letters from various inventors, letters from spirits, philosophical letters. Yesterday an American wrote to ask if I would allow him to baptize a racehorse with my name.'

A LETTER FROM MARIE TO HER BROTHER JOZEF IN 1904.

HIDDEN DANGERS!

Early on in its discovery, Pierre had strapped a small phial containing radium to his arm. He recorded the subsequent burns he received and how long they took to heal. If radium destroyed living skin cells, perhaps it could be used to kill diseased cells, too. These findings led other physicians to experiment using radium as a cure for cancer. Radium became the next 'big thing' and up until the 1920s, radium cures were linked to easing anything from stomach troubles to diseases such as arthritis. Such cures seem madness now because we know that if it is used in the wrong way, radium and radiation can cause cancer. But at that time people were unaware of the dangers of radioactivity, and nobody more so than the Curies.

IN THEIR OWN WORDS

'The ends of fingers that had held tubes or capsules containing very active products became hard and sometimes very painful. For one of us the inflammation… lasted fifteen days and ended with the shedding of the skin, but the pain has not disappeared after two months.'

ENTRY BY PIERRE CURIE IN THE LABORATORY NOTEBOOKS, IN ABOUT 1901.

Marie and Pierre spent hours in their little laboratory working with pure radioactive materials without any protection. By 1902 they both suffered from aches, pains and tiredness. Marie lost weight, but they blamed it on eating too little and overworking. Animals in the laboratory died after exposure to radium.

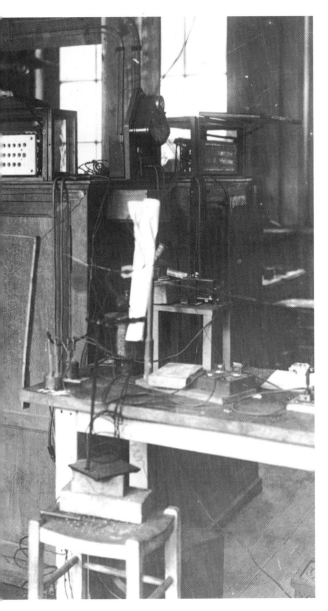

LEFT: *The strain in Marie's eyes shows in this picture taken in 1910. After more than a decade of working with radioactive substances, Marie was often tired and plagued by mystery ailments.*

IN THEIR OWN WORDS

'I am happy with all my injury. My wife is as pleased as I... these are the little accidents of the laboratory.'

PIERRE CURIE, TALKING ABOUT THE 'BURNS' ON HIS HANDS
IN *LA LIBERTÉ* NEWSPAPER, 1903.

In August 1903, Marie miscarried a child and spent months getting better. Later in the year, both Marie and Pierre had been too ill to collect their Nobel Prize. The warning signals had been there but nobody, especially the Curies, wanted to believe that radioactivity could be harmful to people's health.

RIGHT: *Cures and curls! An advertisement for perms from 1924 shows how the radium craze even hit the beauty industry.*

Our New Radium $5.00 Permanent Wave Beauty

COPYRIGHT
1924
H.W. CHERRY

Joy and Despair

IN DECEMBER 1904, Marie gave birth to a healthy baby daughter, called Eve. The Curies had spent a quiet summer in a farmhouse in rural France, away from Paris and all the fuss that the Nobel Prize had brought. After her miscarriage a year earlier, Marie was careful not to work too hard during her pregnancy. But once Eve was born, she was soon back at the laboratory and teaching again. Fortunately for the little girls, Pierre's father lived with them in their flat in Paris. He was very good with his granddaughters and was a big part of their lives while their parents worked.

Pierre became Professor of Physics at the Sorbonne at long last, which meant that he had his own laboratory and Marie became his paid assistant. However by 1905, Pierre found himself unable to work in the laboratory for lengthy periods. The violent pains in his hands and legs had been diagnosed as rheumatism, but medicines didn't help. He was also increasingly tired and long hours stooped over laboratory tables were no longer possible.

In June 1905, the Curies were finally able to go to Sweden to accept their Nobel Prize for Physics. Pierre gave a lecture about radioactivity, but it was his thankyou speech that has been remembered the most. In it, he warns that in the wrong hands, radium could become very dangerous, and a terrible means of destruction.

BELOW: *In between discovering polonium and radium, and bringing up her daughter, Marie still had time to teach. She's pictured here (centre, back row) with her graduates of science, in 1904.*

Happy Days

The summer of 1905, was a happy one. The whole family spent weeks at the seaside and did ordinary things like crabbing and going for long walks. Marie always worried about the health of her family, particularly as her girls did seem to experience lots of childhood illnesses. But, despite Pierre's pains and tiredness, she felt that everybody was doing well that summer. She didn't realize that in less than a year her world would fall apart.

LEFT: *A frail-looking Marie holds one-year-old Eve, with Irène at her side. Despite the solemn expressions, 1905 was a good year for the Curies.*

TRAGEDY STRIKES

It was a wet Easter in 1906 and Paris had just experienced yet more showers. Pierre had just eaten lunch with a group of science professors. He had been in a good mood and had invited them back for dinner at home later that evening to continue their lively discussions. The rain had been lashing down and Pierre hurried through the streets with his umbrella to visit his publisher. Perhaps he was in such a good mood that he simply didn't see the horse-drawn wagon. Or maybe he was tired, and didn't think to look as he quickly crossed the road. Pierre stepped into the path of the horses pulling the wagon. The stunned animals promptly reared as the driver tried to avoid Pierre. In the confusion Pierre fell into the road. The driver couldn't move quickly enough to avoid the back wheel of his wagon hitting Pierre, who died instantly – his skull had been crushed.

LEFT: *Marie never recovered from the loss of Pierre. After his death, she rarely spoke his name.*

Marie was out of town for the day so it was Pierre's father who first received the shocking news. Marie didn't hear until the early evening, when she was plunged into despair and disbelief. She had not only lost a husband she adored but she'd lost the man who had worked by her side every day for eleven years.

The funeral was quiet and Marie watched solemnly. In the following weeks, she received letters from hundreds of admirers and she started a journal in which she wrote to Pierre every day for a year after his death. It was a painful time, but Marie was determined to keep going with her work. Just two weeks after Pierre's death, she was offered his post at the Sorbonne and became the first female professor at the Sorbonne.

IN THEIR OWN WORDS

'My dear Pierre, I want you to know that the laburnum, wisteria and hawthorn are in flower, and the irises are coming out. You would have loved them. I want you to know too that I've been appointed to your chair and some people have been mad enough to congratulate me.'

EXTRACT FROM MARIE'S JOURNAL IN THE YEAR OF PIERRE'S DEATH, 1906.

ABOVE: *Marie lectures on radioactivity at the Sorbonne in 1906. Despite reservations about taking her husband's position, Marie accepted the post so she could continue their work.*

CARRYING ON

After Pierre's death, Marie was left to bring up their children on her own, but she was determined to teach them in the way Pierre and she had often talked about. Rather than send the girls to a school, Marie set up a 'school' of her own made up of friends' children, to make sure they were taught what she wanted. At this time education was concentrated on the classics, whereas Marie wanted her children to learn more about science. She taught the children chemistry, while other parents taught them physics, maths, English, German and geography. Another benefit of her 'school' was the extra time for exercise and sport, which both Marie and Pierre had felt was important to a child's development.

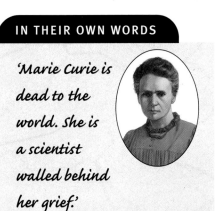

IN THEIR OWN WORDS

'Marie Curie is dead to the world. She is a scientist walled behind her grief.'

FAMILY FRIEND MARGUERITE BOREL, WRITING ABOUT MARIE IN 1910.

BELOW: *The Nobel Prize certificate awarded to Marie in 1911, for her work on radium.*

Meanwhile, in the laboratory, Marie continued her work with radium and polonium. Once again Marie was recognized for her hard work and in 1911, she received the Nobel Prize for Chemistry for her work on radium. Marie made the trip to Stockholm to receive her prize, but she was ill and tired.

The Nature of the Atom

In science circles, the big question of the time was the nature of the atom and how it was structured. Marie's work into radioactivity and radium were important steps in understanding the atom. However in 1913, a scientist from New Zealand called Ernest Rutherford discovered that the atom contained a nucleus. This discovery was the key to understanding nuclear physics.

ABOVE: *Although Marie was not directly involved with the work of Ernest Rutherford, she was interested in his pioneering work and often discussed his discoveries in her own papers.*

UNDERSTANDING THE ATOM

Everything around us is made up of atoms. At their centre is a nucleus, which contains tiny particles, called protons and neutrons. The nucleus is held together by energy. Splitting the nucleus of an atom releases this energy. It is impossible to split the nucleus of most elements , but it is possible with radioactive elements atoms such as uranium and radium. The released energy can be used to make electricity, or it can be used to create explosions, such as in a nuclear bomb. Before radioactivity was discovered, most scientists believed that atoms were the smallest particles.

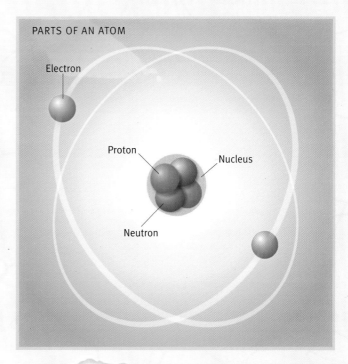

PARTS OF AN ATOM

Electron

Proton

Nucleus

Neutron

MORE PAIN AND LOSS

ABOVE: *Paul Langevin in the 1940s. By 1907, his work on electron theory and magnetism had brought him recognition in physics circles.*

In the years following Pierre's death, Marie became great friends with a scientist called Paul Langevin, whom Pierre had known since 1881. Their friendship developed into a deep love, but Paul was trapped in an unhappy marriage. He wanted to divorce his wife to be with Marie, but in those days it would have caused a great scandal. When Marie and Paul's affair was discovered by the newspapers, they branded Marie a sinful woman, saying that she had tried to tear a father away from his wife and children. The affair was finally brought to an end when private letters between the lovers were leaked to the press by Paul's wife.

In 1911, Marie found herself alone and unpopular with the French public who had once admired her. She became so disliked that some people tried to stop her receiving the Nobel Prize she won that same year. Her health was also getting worse and at one point she became so ill that she was rushed to hospital. Sickness and ill-health dogged Marie for the next two years, and she was unable to work and be part of the great discoveries taking place with radioactivity and the nature of the atom.

Einstein and the Paris Radium Institute

By 1913 Marie was still weak, but looking forward to moving into a new laboratory in Paris, which had been purposely built for research into radium. It would become the Paris Radium Institute. She became friends with the physicist Albert Einstein and shared a walking holiday with his family in the Alps, in Switzerland. Einstein admired Marie's 'sparkling intelligence' and was inspired by her work. They often wrote to each other to discuss science and its effects upon the world. Like Marie, Einstein feared that atomic power would be used in war.

In the summer of 1914, just as life seemed to be getting better for Marie, the First World War began and everyone's lives were turned upside down.

IN THEIR OWN WORDS

'Marie Curie is, of all celebrated beings, the one whom fame has not corrupted.'

ALBERT EINSTEIN

BELOW: *Albert Einstein and his first wife, Mileva. Einstein was a physicist born in Germany, who used maths to prove his theories. He is famous for his theories of relativity, but he also worked on radiation physics. He won the Nobel Prize for Physics in 1921.*

The First World War and Beyond

THE HOT SUMMER of 1914 didn't bring the tourists to Paris. France feared a German invasion and people were leaving the capital. Marie had been concerned about the precious supply of radium in her laboratory and was under orders from the French government to hide it in a safer place outside Paris, where the Germans couldn't lay their hands on it. Marie took the radium on a train packed with soldiers and people moving out of the capital. Then she deposited it in a bank vault in Bordeaux. It must have been nerve-racking for her, but this was to be the first of Marie's many wartime adventures.

BELOW: *Stretcher-bearers heave injured soldiers through the mud during the First World War, in 1917. The senseless loss of life made Marie determined to do something to help.*

'The Little Curie'

Despite her frailty, Marie threw herself into the war effort and championed the cause of injured soldiers. She wanted to find a way of getting X-ray equipment out to wounded French soldiers on the battlefield so that bullets and shrapnel could be easily located and the soldiers operated on quickly and effectively.

Marie masterminded the idea of a vehicle with X-ray equipment. Then she raised the money to make this specialist vehicle, which became known as the 'Little Curie'. By the end of the war, a fleet of eighteen 'Little Curies' had been put together by Marie and her daughter Irène. Marie also helped to set up over 200 X-ray clinics, which involved many train journeys burdened down with heavy X-ray equipment.

Throughout the war, Marie took a hands-on role. She could be found at the front line, helping doctors to X-ray the wounded soldiers, or in Paris, training nurses and other women how to use X-ray equipment. Irène also became a teacher and by the end of the war, the invincible mother-and-daughter team had trained about 150 women to use X-ray equipment.

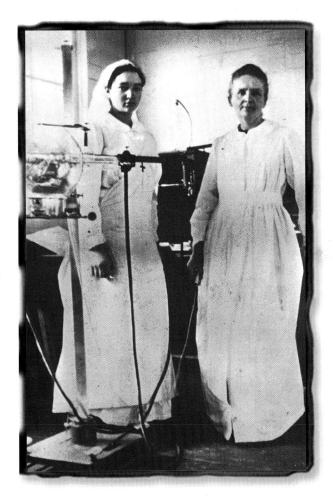

ABOVE: 'You and I, Irène, we will try to make ourselves useful', wrote Marie in 1914. Months later they swapped black dresses for white nursing uniforms. This picture was taken in a Belgian X-ray post in 1915.

THE PARIS RADIUM INSTITUTE

In 1918, after the war had ended, Marie became Director of the Paris Radium Institute. Here she continued her research into radium and its possible uses in science and medicine. By now some people had been cured of cancer using radium treatment.

In 1920, an American journalist called Marie Meloney came to Paris to interview Marie. Nobody had interviewed Marie for years because she had always been publicity shy. At their first meeting, Meloney was moved by the shy little woman wearing black. But what struck her the most was the lack of funding in Marie's laboratories. Meloney was also shocked to find that there was just one gramme of radium in France. She promised Marie that she would go back to the USA and use her female contacts to raise enough money ($100,000) to buy another gramme of radium.

BELOW: *The Paris Radium Institute was founded in 1914. Marie was involved in the design of the building, especially the laboratories. They were large and airy, in stark contrast to the small, badly equipped laboratory where she had first discovered polonium.*

LEFT: *Marie and her daughter Irène stand either side of President Harding at the White House, in Washington DC, USA, in 1921.*

The women became great friends and when Maloney went back to the USA to champion Marie's cause, Marie started to think about visiting the USA for herself.

True to her word, Maloney raised enough money in America to buy a gramme of radium and in 1921, Marie and her two daughters sailed to the USA to receive this precious gift. She was presented with the key for a casket of radium by President Warren Harding at the White House, in Washington DC. Marie attended parties and lectures, but her health was bad. She was partly blind and extremely weak, so she had to return to France early.

IN THEIR OWN WORDS

'I waited a few minutes, in a bare little office which might have been furnished from Grand Rapids, Michigan. Then the door opened and I saw a pale, timid little woman in a black cotton dress, with the saddest face I had ever looked upon... Her kind, patient, beautiful face had the detached expression of a scholar.'

MARIE MALONEY WRITING ABOUT HER FIRST MEETING WITH MARIE IN 1920.

MARIE'S LAST YEARS

From 1918 to 1934, Marie continued to work as Director of the Paris Radium Institute, which expanded to include forty researchers. Marie recruited and taught hundreds of young scientists. She employed many female researchers, too, an unusual step in the 1920s. There were also plans for a hospital and even a processing laboratory, where larger quantities of radioactive substances could be made for use in her laboratories.

Marie also strived to add more radioactive substances to the collection in the Institute. She travelled extensively, and on trips to Italy and Belgium, she gave lectures and raised funds for the Institute.

ABOVE: *The opening of the Warsaw Radium Institute in Poland was one of Marie's greatest personal achievements. It was also a good excuse to visit her friends and relatives in her homeland.*

One of Marie's last great joys was founding a Radium Institute in her home town of Warsaw, in Poland. In 1929, she went back to the USA to collect the money raised for a second gramme of radium, which would be housed in Warsaw. Once again she was welcomed at the White House by a US president, this time President Herbert Hoover.

Sadly, Marie also lived to see the harm caused to humans by radioactive substances. By 1928, fifteen women who had painted watch-dials with luminous paint containing radium had died, and others suffered from anaemia. Young scientists in the Paris Radium Institute died from leukaemia and anaemia. X-ray technicians lost their eyesight or had to have limbs amputated. Marie herself had problems with her eyes and had been plagued by illness for years.

In late 1933, at the age of sixty-six, Marie was still writing about radioactivity and planning a new home. But early the following year she wasn't strong enough to fight her illness anymore. She was diagnosed with leukaemia, a blood disease which we now know is caused by contact with radioactive substances. She was moved to a hospital in the Swiss mountains, where she battled on for a few months. On 4 July 1934, with her daughter Eve at her side, she died quietly.

RIGHT: *Neither fatigue, nor even cataracts over her eyes, could stop Marie working. In her last years, she still worked in her laboratory through the night, often with her daughter Irène at her side.*

IN THEIR OWN WORDS

'*Life is not easy for any of us. But what of that? We must have perseverance and above all confidence in ourselves. We must believe that we are gifted for something, and that this thing, at whatever cost, must be attained.*'

MARIE CURIE, DISCUSSING LIFE AND SCIENCE.

The Legacy of Marie Curie

MARIE FEARED THAT her discovery of radium and the nature of radioactivity would be used in war. Fortunately she didn't live to see this happen. Nuclear weapons were first used in 1945, in the Second World War, when the USA dropped a nuclear bomb on the city of Hiroshima in Japan. A few days later a second bomb was dropped on the city of Nagasaki. Both cities were destroyed and 166,000 people died. The dreadful radiation sickness experienced by people who survived the impact of the bomb revealed the potential harm to humans of radioactive substances. One of the terrible effects of radiation is cancer and years later, a higher-than-average number of people suffer from cancer in these places.

BELOW: *A mushroom cloud develops over a nuclear bomb detonated during tests over the Pacific in 1967. Since the bomb was first used in the Second World War, the threat of nuclear war has hovered ominously over everyone's heads.*

But Marie's research led to many good things. Unlike the Curies, scientists who work in radioactive environments now wear protective clothing and masks. Radioactive substances can be used in nuclear power stations to create electricity. With the world's major sources of fuel for electricity (coal, oil and gas) in danger of running out, nuclear power plays a big part in supplying our future energy needs.

Despite their dangers, Marie's discoveries have benefitted medicine, particularly cancer treatment. In the late 1990s, over 400 people worked in the research department of the Paris Radium Institute and 900 in its medical division. In a typical year there are over 70,000 consultations and 6,000 patients treated in this institute alone. Throughout the world, radiotherapy is used to treat millions of sick people.

In April 1995, President François Mitterrand believed it was time Marie and Pierre were buried in a place befitting two of the country's greatest scientists. Their ashes were laid to rest at the Panthéon in Paris, a monument to French heroes and other famous people. Over 100 years had passed since a shy young Polish woman had boarded a train to this great city. Now she had finally received its greatest honour.

ABOVE: *The coffins of Marie and Pierre during a memorial ceremony at the Panthéon in Paris. Marie is the first woman to be buried in the Panthéon, alongside France's 'great men'.*

BELOW: *Most hospitals now boast a radiology department. Radiotherapy is one of our most effective treatments against cancer.*

Timeline

1803

John Dalton (1766-1844), an English chemist, presents the theory that chemical elements are made of atoms.

1864

Louis Pasteur (1822-1895) discovers that organisms in the air cause milk to go sour.

1865

Sir Joseph Lister (1827-1912) introduces antiseptics after realizing that the formation of pus is due to germs.

1869

Dmitri Mendeleev and Julius Lothar Meyer group elements with similar properties in the periodic law.

1867

7 NOVEMBER: Marya Sklodowska is born in Warsaw, Poland.

1874

Marya's sister Zofia dies of typhus.

1876

Alexander Graham Bell (1847-1922) invents the telephone.

1877

Thomas Alva Edison invents the phonograph.

1878

Marya's mother dies from tuberculosis. Louis Pasteur discovers streptococcus bacteria.

1883

Marya finishes her school education and stays with relatives on a farm for a year.

1885

Marya returns to Warsaw and becomes a governess. Louis Pasteur uses a rabies vaccine for the first time, saving a boy's life.

1888

The Pasteur Institute is founded in Paris, for the study, prevention, and treatment of disease, in recognition of the work of Louis Pasteur.

1889

The Eiffel Tower is built.

1891

Marya moves to Paris and changes her name to Marie. She starts studying at the Sorbonne, the University of Paris.

1893

Marie graduates with a physics degree.

1894

Marie meets Pierre Curie, and graduates with a maths degree.

1895

26 JULY: Marie and Pierre get married. Wilhelm Röntgen discovers X-rays.

1896

Charles Laveran (1845–1922), a French physician, discovers the parasite that causes malaria.

1897
SEPTEMBER: Irène Curie is born.
DECEMBER: Marie begins to
research radium rays.

1898
Marie and Pierre Curie
discover polonium and radium.
Marie invents the word
'radioactive', to describe any
material that gives off strange rays.

1900
Population of Paris: 2.7 million
(larger than New York or Berlin)

1902
Marie and Pierre isolate
pure radium.

1903
JUNE: Marie gains a Ph.D. in
Physics, from the Sorbonne.
NOVEMBER: Marie and Pierre
Curie, along with Antoine Henri
Becquerel (1852-1908) are
awarded the Nobel Prize for
Physics for discovering
radioactivity and for their work
on uranium.
Marie and Pierre win the Davy
Medal, for their discovery
of radium.
AUGUST: Marie has a miscarriage.

1904
DECEMBER: Eve Curie is born.

1906
APRIL: Pierre Curie is killed by a
horse-drawn wagon in Paris.
Marie becomes the first female
professor at the Sorbonne.

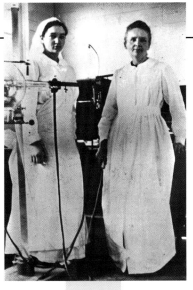

1908
Gabriel Lippmann (1845-1921)
wins the Nobel Prize for Physics
for his method of colour
photography.

1910
Marie establishes the melting
point of polonium.

1911
Marie Curie is awarded the
Nobel Prize for Chemistry, for
her work on radium.

1913
Ernest Rutherford (1871-1937)
discovers that the atom
contains a nucleus.

1914
Marie helps to found the Paris
Radium Institute.
First World War begins. Marie
carries a supply of radium out of
Paris and stores it in Bordeaux.
She helps the war effort by
becoming a nurse with her
daughter Irène, and develops the
'Little Curie' X-ray vehicle.

1918
First World War ends. Marie
becomes the first Director of the
Paris Radium Institute.

1920
Marie Meloney interviews
Marie Curie in Paris.

1921
Marie and her daughter Irène
travel to the USA to receive a
gramme of radium from President
Harding at the White House.

1929
Marie returns to the USA to
collect a second gramme of
radium for the Warsaw
Radium Institute.

1934
4 JULY: Marie is diagnosed as
suffering from leukaemia. She dies
in a hospital in Switzerland.

1995
APRIL: The ashes of Marie and
Pierre Curie are buried at the
Panthéon, in Paris, after a special
ceremony led by President
François Mitterand.

Glossary

atoms
The small particles that make up every chemical element.

chaperone
Somebody who looks after a younger person when they go out anywhere in public.

classics
Ancient Greek and Latin, literature and history.

compound
A mixture of two or more things. In science, a compound is made up of two or more elements.

diagnosed
When a doctor has discovered what is wrong with a patient.

distilled
Purified. Substances are usually distilled by heating them up and then cooling them down, collecting the pure liquid or solid that remains.

electrolyzed
A substance that has been broken down by having electricity passed through it.

element
A pure substance, which cannot be broken down to make other substances.

emission
Something that is given off by a substance, such as rays, light, sound or heat.

Humphry Davy Medal
A medal given to scientists in memory of Sir Humphry Davy (1778–1829), the English chemist who invented the miner's lamp.

isolate
To separate something into its pure form.

journal
A daily record, such as a diary.

melting point
The temperature at which something begins to melt.

Nobel Prize
The Nobel Prize was the idea of the Swedish chemist, Alfred B. Nobel (1833–96), who left money to fund the awards in his will. Founded in 1901, the prize is awarded to people who have made outstanding contributions in the fields of physics, chemistry, medicine, literature, world peace and economics.

nuclear
To do with the nucleus, or core of an atom.

nuclear bomb
A bomb that uses the energy created by splitting the nucleus of an atom to create an explosion.

phosphorescence
A light given off by certain substances.

physicist
A professional person who is trained in physics, the science of energy and matter.

properties
In science, this means the characteristics of a substance, for example, whether it gives off phosphorescence or heat.

radioactive
A substance that gives off dangerous rays.

radiotherapy
The treatment of disease using X-rays or radiation.

shrapnel
Pieces of metal that fly off bombs when they explode.

sociology
The study of how humans live together in society.

X-rays
A penetrating form of radiation, which can pass through something solid.

Further Information

BOOKS FOR YOUNGER READERS

Groundbreakers: Marie Curie
by Ann Fullick (Heinemann, 2000)

Energy Forever: Nuclear Power
by Ian Graham (Hodder Wayland, 1998)

Famous Lives: Scientists
by Nina Morgan (Wayland, 1993)

Get a Life!: Marie Curie
by Philip Ardagh (Macmillan, 2000)

Livewire Real Lives: Marie Curie
(Hodder and Stoughton Educational, 2000)

Science Discoveries: Marie Curie and Radium
by Steve Parker (Belitha, 1992)

Super Scientists: The Mysterious Element,
The Story of Marie Curie
by Pam Robson (Hodder Wayland, 1997)

BOOKS FOR OLDER READERS

Grand Obsession: Madame Curie and Her World
by Rosalynd Pflaum (Doubleday, 1989)

Marie Curie: A Biography
by Eve Curie (Da Capo, 1986). This was first
published in 1937 and is a classic work.

Marie Curie: A Life
by Susan Quinn (Heinemann, 1995)

Paris on the Eve: 1900–1914
by Vincent Cronin (Collins, 1989)

Victorian Women
by Joan Perkin (John Murray, 1993)

WEBSITES

American Institute of Physics
www.aip.org
Information and exhibitions about Curie and
other scientists.

Nobel e-Museum
www.nobel.se
The official site of the Nobel Foundation.
Use the search tool to find out about Marie
Curie and other Nobel prize-winners.

ORGANIZATIONS

Marie Curie Cancer Care
28 Belgrave Square
London SW1X 8DG

Index

Page numbers in **bold** are pages where there is a photograph or an illustration.